How Not to Worry!

by Robert Hale

Published by
AVICENNA
C/ R. Curtoys Gotarredona, 1, Esc. 2, 2B
07840 Santa Eulària des Riu
Spain

ISBN: 978-84-120109-4-7

Contents

How Not to Worry!

1. Why Worry?

I bet you were thinking I was going start by telling you how bad worrying was. Ah ha! How wrong you were! I'll save that for later. Worry is good! That is, if looked at from a certain point of view (and looking at things from different points of view is one thing you are going to have to learn to do!). If you all didn't worry, humankind would long ago have been wiped out. By a pandemic (we have one as I write), a nuclear war, being eaten by sabre-toothed tigers, or poisoned from eating toxic plants or from taking dangerous medicines willy nilly. So to worry is in our nature.

And in our nurture. That is, whether we worry a lot or not is influenced not only by our genes, but also by our upbringing, our culture, and our experiences, especially early ones. It is even influenced by how anxious our mothers were when we were still in her womb.

Now I have to say something not all of you may like to listen to. The thing is, women worry, men act. Now before (if you are of the female sex/gender/self-identification) you start tweeting for bad things to happen to me (I do not have a Twitter account by the way), let me moderate that a little. It's a matter of percentages. I am going to be careful how I put this, and as I am making the effort to do so, I would like you to be careful how you read it. Here goes: There is a greater tendency to worry among the population of women than among the population of men. There, did you get that? It is not saying that because you personally are a woman, you are a worrier, just that on average you stand a greater chance of being a person who worries more. And this is not just a swivel-eyed idea of mine, it has actually been shown by proper research[1].

The other bit (men act) may prove a little less defensible. A woman friend of mine (yes, I have them) agreed with me that women worry more, but she opined that this was because men were too lazy. That is in direct opposition to the second part of my theory. Or it would be if we did not use the cunning device of saying that "to act" refers to a spectrum of acting, from a minimum (zero) to a maximum degree of acting, and so it includes being lazy. But let me instead artfully change tack and reveal that what I really meant by "act" is "to engage in problem-focused, task-oriented coping". That means to regard a challenging situation not as something to worry over, but as a problem to be

---

1 Robichaud M et al. 2003. Gender differences in worry and associated cognitive-behavioral variables. Journal of Anxiety Disorders, Volume 17, Issue 5, 2003, pages 501-516.

solved. Men are more inclined to do this, and there is research evidence for this too[2].

My further contention is that this is biological. When humankind was living in caves it made sense for our survival to have different classes of people engaged in different roles, and (to mother nature or to unreconstructed men, as you please) it seemed like a good idea *at the time* (please note that I said that!) to have this split organised on gender lines. The men, being bigger and stronger, would go to hunt bison, wage war, and fight off rampaging sabre-toothed tigers. The women, who had the babies, would nurse them, look after the children, make the home and do the sewing, cooking and washing up.

Now, psychologists know that reduced control leads to more worry. So while the men were away doing man stuff, the women, left sitting at home or venturing out a little way to gather berries, not having the same level of control over their destiny that the men had, would worry. Which, furthermore, was also useful. Small children are especially vulnerable and need to be protected, which requires a sensitive appreciation of potential danger rather than idle complacency. It was useful

2   Lipińska-Grobelny A et al. 2011. Effects of gender role on personal resources and coping with stress. International Journal of Occupational Medicine and Environmental Health, Volume 24, pages 18–28.

also in stirring the men to action when they were lying about the cave ("Uleg! For the Great Sun God's sake, get up off your lazy **se, pick up that spear and go and do the weekly. Don't you realise we're down to our last leg of woolly mammoth, you loafing sloth?!"). Well, I have witnessed pre-agricultural villagers when the men were at home, and that, I am ashamed to confess, is what they do. Lie around. While the women work.

So, worry is good. There is nothing *wrong* with it. To a degree. But beyond that degree, it is bad. Worrying a lot is called anxiety. In the long-term anxiety has been shown to be bad for you. Anxiety may increase your risk of depression, asthma, gastrointestinal disturbances like irritable bowel syndrome, cardiovascular diseases like high blood pressure, heart disease and strokes, infections (through reduced immunity), and neurological degenerative diseases. It is bad for your health, your longevity and your quality of life.

Also, whether worry is healthy or not depends on the context. If something serious is happening right now which threatens the life, health or security of you or your loved ones right now, it is normal and even healthy to worry somewhat. So long as that worry acts as a call to some useful action. That action might be to provide a sympathetic ear, comfort or offer to help out a family member, a relative or friend. It might be to take action to modify the situation such that it becomes less serious. Or it might be to get the hell out of there. Any of these may be an appropriate response depending on the context. Or not.

But, just for example, if something is not happening now that threatens you and yours, it's just that you think it might at some time in the future, but in your mind you grossly inflate the chance that it might by obsessively thinking about it, and you react - not to any actual happening, but to your imaginings about a hypothetical - by flying into a fearful, tearful whirlwind of panic, that is not good, healthy, or useful! Obviously I have described an extreme. There are gradations of not good below this. But it's really quite simple: you know when your worry is not good because it doesn't feel nice and it's not doing any good.

Apart from its more obvious effects on your physical health and mental well-being, worrying is a huge drain on and misuse of your valuable energy, that should rightly be used for useful or fulfilling things like learning, creating, problem-solving and loving. If you are able to focus on the object of your worry, that is proof that you are skilled at focusing, right? But you are focusing on the wrong thing, or on the right thing in the wrong way.

Worrying is also a tragic waste of precious time. We are not immortal beings. We are less than an instant in the great mystery of our universe. We will die, all too soon. There is no guarantee you will be living an hour from now. Don't waste whatever time you have left in worrying, use it well.

Further, worrying about something can sometimes actually make the thing you are worried about happen. If you worry too much that you will make lots of mistakes during your driving test, you probably will. If you worry that you have eaten too many calories today according to your diet, you may just say, "Oh well, I might as well really blow it now!", and gorge yourself. If you worry that your lack of muscular armature makes you look silly, you might go to a gym and pump iron until you gain so much muscle you really do look silly. If you worry about getting ill, you could end up making yourself ill. If you worry about failure, you might not try, or you might not try what it takes to succeed. You would miss out on the fantastic opportunity which comes with every so-called 'failure' to learn a valuable life lesson, a lesson which might have helped you eventually to succeed in ways you had never envisaged.

If you want to worry less, mark well what Rudolf Abel says to James Donovan in *The Bridge of Spies* when the latter, surprised by Abel's calmness in the face of a potential conviction for spying and a death sentence, asks him if he is not worried...

"Would it do any good?"

Main Points

- Worry is in our nature and our nurture.

- It has a biological function.

- But it can be excessive or inappropriate.

- Excessive worry is a massive waste of precious energy and time.

- Think: "Is it doing any good?"

How Not to Worry?

2. Worry Goblins

Worry begins with a negative thought. For some people, and the chances are you are one of them if you are reading this book, negative thoughts are a habit.

Whoa!!! What do you mean by negative? Do you mean, like, *bad*? No, not *bad*, just bad. Not morally or ethically wrong. No judgement intended. Just bad as in not useful and potentially harmful to you.

But don't worry, those habits are caused by goblins and you have the power to take *their* power away! Let me introduce you to some worry goblins and tell you what you have to do to disempower them.

Empty Glass Goblin

Empty Glass has a couple of tricks. It can make you see only the negative side of any situation ("My glass is half empty"). Or it can make you choose to deny or minimise any positive side even when you do see it.

Say to this goblin: I know what you're doing and this is a deceitful scam. I'm going to ignore you and look on the bright side.

Catastrophe Goblin

Catastrophe Goblin loves to make mountains out of a molehills and storms in teacups. It makes you see problems as being very much more important or difficult than they really are.

Say to this goblin: You are wildly exaggerating as always. Stop it and go away.

Spilled-Milk Goblin

Spilled-Milk Goblin (obviously) cries over spilled milk. It is best friends with Catastrophe Goblin.

Say to this goblin: What's happened is over and done with. There's nothing to be done about it now. So scram!

Negative Assumption Goblin

This little blighter always assumes something negative about any situation. For instance, your partner goes hiking and they are not back by five minutes before they said they would, so you think they must have been eaten by sabre-toothed tigers. Or something.

Tell this goblin: Why on Earth are you thinking that? There's very little chance of him having been eaten. There are several infinitely more probable possibilities. Go away while I think of the most likely.

Doomsayer Goblin

A close cousin of Negative Assumption Goblin, it likes to make pessimistic predictions based on its prejudice or your fears. According to this goblin any act or enterprise is always doomed to failure, and in any case tomorrow bad things are bound to happen.

Say: You are unbelievable! You have absolutely no evidence for that! Away with you this instant!

Black and White Goblin

Black and White makes you think that things are clear-cut and opposed to each other when the reality is much more complex. It thinks in all-or-nothing terms of extremes with no middle ground. Example: "If you're not with me, you must be against me".

Say: *You* may be colour blind but *I* am not!

Pigeonhole Goblin

PH Goblin (for short) likes to label other people on a pretty arbitrary basis. It is a close cousin of Black and White Goblin. PG Goblin says things like, "There are two kinds of people in the world, etc. etc." But it has prejudices too. Just say you have formed the impression that a colleague is a bad mother just because she has a tattoo on her arm. If so, Pigeonhole Goblin is in your head!

Tell it: Listen! Life and people are a *tiny* bit more complex than that, you Dodo. And don't judge a book by its cover!

Sweeping Generalisation Goblin

SG Goblin makes you generalise inappropriately. For example, if you think the whole world is bad because the world contains some bad people, SG Goblin has been getting at you.

Tell it: You are not being rational. That doesn't follow at all.

Selective Vision Goblin

SV Goblin makes you see the side of things which confirm what you already believe. If you believe you are not well liked, then you see two of your workmates talking together and one of them glances towards you, so you conclude they must have been talking unkindly about you, SV Goblin has been at work.

Say: Let's think of some alternative explanations shall we? And weigh up the evidence before jumping to conclusions!

Musturbator Goblin

Musturbator[3] becomes angry or frustrated if things don't happen as they should by rights or morality. It might, for instance, become all upset and indignant and complain loudly if the service in a restaurant is only average, or if it has to stand in a queue for too long at the post office.

Say: You can't expect everything to happen exactly as *you* like it. Don't be judgemental, soften up, be kind!

Perfectionist Goblin

Perfectionist Goblin is a real slave-driver. It wants you to believe that only absolute perfection is acceptable, and that you are uniquely responsible for correcting the imperfections around you. It makes you believe you will not be valued if you do not achieve and maintain impossibly high standards. It forces you to take an inordinate amount of time over any task in order to correct tiny unimportant details.

Tell it: Listen! You are a liar. First of all, I am not so important that everything I do needs to be perfect. Second, you call out so-called "defects" which do not matter. Third, the world is untidy and I am not bound to hold it to your standards, which

---

3 "Musturbation" is a term coined by the psychologist Albert Ellis.

in any case, are beginning to look a little ridiculous. Fourth, the best people value me for my *human qualities*, not my abilities and my work ethic. Fifth, "the perfect is the enemy of the good"[4]. Sixth, loosen up, be kind, and get a life!

Ruminator Goblin

Ruminator makes you recycle your worrying thought endlessly. It makes you think about it over and over again. Over and over and over and over and over and over and over.... Well, I think you get the picture.

Say: I acknowledge your presence but I am not going to attach any importance to it. I am going to let you go out of my head just as you came in, and I am going to focus my attention on something else something more pleasant or funny or uplifting. And if you come in again, I'll do the same.

Obsessive Goblin

Obsessive Goblin makes you do things... uhm... obsessively. It is a sibling of Perfectionist and Ruminator. If you like sport, it makes your sport take over your life, to the detriment of other areas of your life and even your health. In the end, your sport becomes a chore rather than an enjoyment.

---

4   To paraphrase Voltaire.

And the same with anything else: studying, fishing, healthy eating, doing puzzles, and so on.

Say to it: It's time to realise you're going too far. There's no need for this. This routine is killing me. I'm not going to listen to you any more. I'm going to break this routine right now and forever.

Not Enough Time Goblin

Makes you believe you have to do everything today.

Tell it: Calm down! Listen, there are things that are urgent, things that are important but not urgent, and things that are neither. The things that are urgent are the only ones I need to do today. And actually there is only one of them. The important things I can do tomorrow. The others... well, they don't really have to be done at all!

Stone-Throwing Goblin

ST Goblin makes you blameless. It blames all bad things on others: other people, your tools, the government, Murphy (of the eponymous law), God, etc. It never lets you take any blame, or any responsibility.

Tell it: You don't always have to find someone or something to blame. And sometimes you have to let me accept responsibility for my own part. I would be a bigger person for that, not a smaller one.

All-About-You Goblin

Turns all conversation around to you and your exploits, and makes you take all things personally. It wields a double-edged sword which, while it always lays blame on you, also gives you all the credit.

Say: For goodness sake can't you see what you're doing? You really need to drop this self-importance! Here is a mantra: "I am no more nor less worthy of attention than anybody else on the planet".

Always Right Goblin

Always Right Goblin makes you believe you are diminished if you are wrong or make a mistake. It makes you argumentative.

Say: Does it really matter? I would rather be happy than right!

Always Wrong Goblin

Always Wrong Goblin makes you believe you will be more highly valued if you accept you are in error. It is always making you apologise for things which are not your fault.

Tell it: I don't need this hassle. Let me think about this for a second. Is this *really* my fault? If it isn't there is no need for me to feel in the wrong. I think you are lying, but if anyone will only value me if they can subdue my spirit, they'll have to think again.

There are more goblins, but I think these are the main ones. Do you recognise any of them? I bet you recognise at least one, probably two or three.

But how do the goblins make you worry? They do this by making a bad feeling. About yourself, undermining your confidence or your self-esteem; about other people, thereby creating a sense of anger, conflict, or cynicism; and about the world, again generating anger, cynicism or despair. If they do this often enough, your negative feelings become negative attitudes, and negative attitudes in turn can generate an anxious predisposition. That means you're more likely to worry. In time it becomes a habit. Because every negative thought you have reinforces negativity.

Let me just go through that again:

Negative thoughts → Negative feelings → Negative attitudes → More likely to worry → The worry habit

Don't Feed the Goblins!

What do worry goblins feed on? Four main things: Pessimism, fear, ingrained beliefs, and self-importance. Different goblins feed on these things in different amounts. For instance, Doomsayer loves pessimism, Ruminator binges on fear, Pigeonhole eats ingrained beliefs for breakfast, and Perfectionist would wither and fade without self-importance. I will say just a little about each of these.

Pessimism

Remember Eeyore, the depressive donkey in the Winnie the Pooh books? He is a pessimist. Like Eeyore, pessimists think the worst of everything, basically meaning the future and the world. Are you one? If you are, you may have said to somebody once, "I'm not a pessimist, I'm a realist!" But are you? Think of this: in the foreseeable future very bad and very good things are statistically much much less likely to happen than ordinary things. So if you think bad things will always happen, you are not being a realist, you are being wrong! And what about this realism: statistically, optimists are more likely to be happier, healthier, wealthier, and longer lived. That or a "realist"? I know which I'd rather be!

Fear

Fear is good in the short term, for example if suddenly confronted by a sabre-toothed tiger while out gathering berries. But if fear becomes a habit, if you are constantly afraid that a sabre-toothed tiger might drag your children out of your cave one night and eat them, even though no sabre-toothed tigers had been seen in the area for the past twenty years, that fear is not doing you any good. Look it in the eye, tell it it is out of order, and to come back only when you need it.

Ingrained beliefs

We may not even know we have them, but it is worth asking ourselves the question: What caused me to think or to say what I just thought or said? There must be some broader belief behind it. What is it exactly? This requires a modicum of self-awareness. Self-awareness (not self-obsession, mark you!) is a commodity you will need if you want to stop worrying.

An example may help. During hard times it is easy to believe that somebody or something (God, the world, the universe, etc.) has got it in for us, or that we were "born unlucky". Some people go through life saying to themselves, "I am unlucky". That is an ingrained belief. That belief leads to a vicious cycle of self-pity, fatalism, believing it's not worth the effort, not looking for solutions, further failure, and so on. This conditions the person's thoughts and words. They will not rise to a challenge because they will say to themselves, "It's not worth it, I am unlucky and the world is against me". If the person who believes they are unlucky does not begin to change that belief, they will go on hexing themselves for the rest of their lives. They will be constantly frustrated, anxious and unhappy. And unlucky.

Nobody likes to give up their beliefs easily. But faced with the firm possibility that they may be feeding our goblins, we must recognise them and look at them critically. In order to challenge our beliefs, we need to be flexible.

Self-importance

We are all attached to our sense of self-importance. That is, we love to be praised and we don't like to be criticised. We want to be right, we don't want to be shown to be wrong. To some, this is so important that it causes anxiety or conflict or both, and therefore worry. It is an extraordinary waste of energy maintaining the image of ourselves we wish others to see. We need to get rid of our self-importance, while maintaining our self-belief. Do not be over-affected by either praise or criticism. They should not be so important to your own self-belief. You can be yourself better than anybody else in the world, but you are only one in seven and a half billion. You are small and the universe is big. But you are all that you see, and you have a universe inside you. Remember that mantra: "I am no more nor less worthy than anybody else on the planet". (OK, you may say the President of the

United States is more important than you, but we are talking about inner worth here!)

Let me now introduce some allies to cultivate...

Your Allies

Remember this:

Negative thoughts → Negative feelings → Negative attitudes → More likely to worry → The worry habit

It works the other way round too:

Positive thoughts → Positive feelings → Positive attitudes → Less likely to worry → The happy habit

Every positive thought you have reinforces the happy habit.

You need to rework your thoughts, replacing negative with positive, and you need some allies to help you. They will help you make your thoughts more positive, kinder, more realistic and more helpful. The new way of thinking will slowly but surely become part of your universe. Your allies are...

- Flexibility
- Self-awareness
- Reason
- Clarity
- Kindness
- Optimism
- Humility
- Self-belief

Main Points

- There are many goblins which give you negative thoughts.

- Negative thoughts generate worry.

- You can choose to call the goblins out and have a positive thought instead of a negative one.

- Goblins feed on pessimism, fear, ingrained beliefs and self-importance.

- You can recognise and challenge these things.

- Cultivate your thought allies.

3. How to Stop Worrying

Here's how...

Breathe

Meditate

Exercise

Distract your mind

Slow down!

Get in touch with nature

Be practical

Rationalise

Talk to people

Change your mind

Nurture self-belief

If you practise these things often enough, believe me, you *will* worry less! It is inevitable!

Breathe

What's the most important thing you can do for your health right now? You got it! But you must do it right. I can see you now. I can see the muscles at the front of your neck are tight, they have your upper ribs jammed up in an elevated position, which means your lungs are half full of stale air before you even start to breath in. You haven't got too much more capacity so your breathing is shallow. To compensate for that it's also too fast. That way of breathing makes your blood more alkaline, ever so slightly but enough to make you more anxious. It also changes your posture. It's part of the "worry posture", the unconscious perception of which feeds back into your subconscious mind making you worry even more.

Now, lie down on your back and follow these instructions:

1. Begin to breathe calmly with your abdomen. You can check this by placing a hand lightly on your tummy.

2. Make your breathing just a little slower than normal.

3. As you breathe out do not blow the air out forcefully, just let it flow out naturally.

4. Make your out-breath slightly longer than your in-breath. During your in-breath, count in seconds: "One, two, three", then breathe out: "...four, five, six, seven".

5. At the end of your out-breath pause for a fraction of a second before beginning your next in-breath.

6. Don't count the seconds any more, see if you can maintain the rhythm without having to count.

7. Now on your out-breath, mentally (not vocally) say to yourself "Relax...".

I want you to practice like this for five minutes every day.

Meditate

Meditation isn't just for yogis, hippies and people who live in Glastonbury, it is for people like you*!

You can do it anywhere but it's better outside or at least with the window open if it's not too cold. You can also do it in any position but lying on your back or sitting are best. If lying down, you can use a pillow under your head and another under your knees if it's more comfortable. If seated, don't slouch but don't worry about your posture. Just be comfortable.

Now, get into position, get comfortable, close your eyes, settle, breath as above a few times. Then, what you'll have to do is focus on your sensations instead of your thoughts. Or, in other words, let sensations displace your thoughts. Feel your breath going in then going out. Can you feel your heart beating? Feel your weight against the surface you are lying or sitting on. If you are outside or have the window open, can you feel a breeze on your skin? Can you feel the sun on your body? Do you feel warm? Cold? What else can you feel? What can you hear? Bird song? Traffic noise? Voices? The wind in the trees? Distant thunder? It doesn't matter, just focus your attention on it for a while. Can you smell anything? Coffee? Polish? Flowers? Perfume? Wine? Anything at all? Anything that you feel, hear, smell, do not judge. Do not say, "This is good" or, "This is bad", just observe it with curiosity. If thoughts come into your mind, do the same. Observe their presence but do not think *about* them. Then let them go and feel, hear and smell. Five minutes is enough. Then bring yourself back to normal awareness and open your eyes.

There! You have just done what is called mindfulness meditation. I'd like you to practice this once a day*.

*UNLESS (AND THIS IS IMPORTANT)...

... you currently or at any time have suffered from: bipolar disorder, schizophrenia, psychosis, major depressive disorder or suicidal ideas.

... you are currently affected by severe emotional trauma, active addiction/substance abuse, recent bereavement, or insulin-dependent diabetes.

In all these cases **check with your doctor** before doing mindfulness meditation.

Exercise

Mens sana in corpore sano: "A healthy mind in a healthy body". Everybody without exception should do some regular exercise, adapted to their age and state of health. Moderate, low-impact, aerobic exercise (walking, gentle jogging, cycling, swimming, moderate intensity workouts) is best. High impact, high intensity activities or obsessive exercising are not good. Exercise clears your lungs out, fills your blood with oxygen, gets your blood circulating, distracts your mind, gets endorphins (the happy hormones) circulating, and improves your mood. If you're a natural couch potato, get up off your backside and give it a go. You never know you might actually like it! I've seen many converts, and that's because once you feel how good it makes you feel, you won't look back. Three times a week would be good, or even two. But don't obsess and don't beat yourself up if you miss a session. Relax!

IMPORTANT: Talk to your doctor before starting any new exercise regime.

Distract Your Mind

You have already begun to do this by exercising. Here are some other ways:

- Take more time over your passions (cooking, fishing, birdwatching, music, poetry, watching sport, cinema, woodwork, flower arranging, doing jigsaw puzzles, learning French, ancient Persian literature, basket weaving, archery, tiddlywinks, taxidermy, whatever... It doesn't have to be French).

- If you haven't got a hobby, take one up.

- Doing something expressive is a fantastic way to release negativity in a creative way: writing, painting, pottery, music, singing, potato printing, whatever tickles your pickle.

- Be sociable. Phone people. Meet people. Talk to people.

- Listen to your favourite music, watch films, binge on box sets or TV series.

- Read whatever you like to read. Or discover new things to read.

Slow Down!

You're going way too fast! Modern life channels us into the fast lane. We have to be constantly doing, interacting, communicating, and when we are confronted with an empty slot, we immediately try to fill it, and when we can't we worry. Is that sane? It becomes a habit and we worry if we cannot maintain it. Silly, isn't it?

I realised one day that I had forgotten the sublime pleasure of simply hanging around, chatting to people, going hither and thither without a plan, an aim or a time constraint. Being rather than doing. We have to allow ourselves this. So, please slow down with me, I can't do it all on my own!

Get in Touch with Nature

You may have been doing this already while you have been exercising or distracting your mind. But if not, please do do it as "A GOOD THING TO DO" in itself. Psychologists have found lots of evidence that even small touches of nature bring down stress levels. Things as simple as having plants in your home or workplace, spending time in the garden, or a walk in the park. If you have easy access to the countryside or even the wilderness, so much the better. Less stress, less worry. And nature brings you back to your true self. Look at its beauty, its magnificence, its ability to go on and weather all storms. You are all this. Isn't that an awesome feeling?!

Be Practical

Remember Rudolf Abel's question about worrying at the end of Chapter 1? He asked:

"Would it do any good?"

Worry without action does no good. And once you act, you worry less. And the better you act, the less you need to worry!

So, you have to ask yourself: "This thing that I'm worrying about... is it a problem that can be solved?"

If you answer yes, you should then ask: "Can *I* solve it? If so, how can I do it and what or who do I need for that? If not, who can, and can I ask them, and if so, are they likely to help?"

Do you see what I mean? You have turned something to worry about into a problem to be solved. That way you have turned the tables. It no longer has power over you, you have power over it!

Of course, if in answer to these questions you find that you cannot solve the problem, it still isn't going to help if you worry about it, now is it? But you probably will, so you will have to engage the other strategies in this chapter to stop it.

Rationalise

Come now, you are not being rational. Ha ha... Don't you just hate it when somebody tells you that? But that doesn't mean it isn't true. Be brave... entertain the idea.

And look again at some of the goblins in Chapter 2. Some of them bend the truth outrageously. And in doing so bend your mind from a balanced one into a worried one. To rationalise you have to be sufficiently flexible (flexibility is one of your allies!), humble (another one!), and clear-headed (clarity – another one!) to expose your thoughts to brutal cross-examination. Imagine it's another person, and they had said what your worried mind is thinking. Here are the key questions to ask:

- Is that *really* likely?

- What makes you think so?

- Are those reasons valid?

- Let's try and think of some alternative possibilities?

- Which of the possibilities are most likely?

- Which are least likely?

Talk to People

Don't keep it all bottled up! We are social animals. Communication keeps us healthy. Seek a little help from your friends. Other people can help you rationalise and solve your problems. But not all problems are practical. Many are emotional. Talking to people helps get things off your chest and you can receive comfort and/or moral support. Other people are like soothing sponges and brand new batteries all at the same time: they can diffuse and calm our worries and leave us feeling re-energised.

The right people that is. And herein lies the caveat. A great big one. Do not let people reinforce your own goblins! If they do, change tack, change the subject or change the people. So far as possible avoid negative people like the plague. And only offer emotional support yourself if you are strong enough to do so.

Change Your Mind

Very often people say, "I cannot change. This is just the way I am". That is a lie! It was told to them by Ingrained Belief Goblin (backed up by Can't Be Bothered Goblin, who is not a worry goblin but can stick a spanner in anybody's works never the less). You can change, if you want to and if you work at it. Anybody can.

What I mean by 'change your mind' is 'change your attitude, change the nature of your thoughts'. Negative thoughts are a habit and like any habit you can give them up. Replace them with something positive. Be an alchemist, transform lead into gold! So, how do you go about doing it? The method is very easy. You just have to REST....

Recognise your negative thoughts

Examine them

Stop them

Take control

Recognise your negative thoughts

We have said that you can tell when you're worrying because it doesn't feel good. You feel anxious and there might be physical symptoms you can recognise like raising your shoulders, feeling your heartbeat, feeling a knot in your throat, feeling hot and sweaty, and so on. But what you have to do is recognise the thought connected with that. Try and state it in words. A few examples:

- "Jamie isn't back from his walk yet. Something might have happened to him."

- "There's no money coming in. We won't be able to pay the rent and then we'll be starving on the streets."

- "Ginny didn't look well when I saw her. She must be ill."

- "The stock market's crashed. I've lost all my savings."

- "The company's going under. I'll lose my job, then what?"

- "Things are not right between Bobby and me. He must have a lover. How will it end?"

- "I have so many things to do and I must get them all finished today."

- "Someone might have criticised my comment on Facebook. I must check it immediately!"

- "Somebody insulted me. How terrible! How dare they!"

- "A sabre-toothed tiger might break in and eat my babies."

Examine Them

You need to cross examine your thoughts.

What triggered the thought? What was the situation, or the place, the people, the comments or questions that made you have that thought? Write them down. Over time, is there a pattern?

How realistic is the thought? How likely is the thing you're worried about to actually happen? What evidence do you have? Is that evidence good, or weak, or phony? Are you exaggerating? Is this a real problem or is it an imaginary one? If it's a real problem, is it a practical one you can solve? Is it an emotional one you can seek help or support for?

Stop Them

Once you have got used to doing this, you will be in a position to nip your negative thoughts in the bud. As soon as you feel the amber alarm for negativity STOP, BREATHE, calm and clear your mind, and proceed to...

Take control

Now you can *choose* to replace the negative thought with a positive one...

- "Jamie likes to walk. He can't always judge the time it will take him exactly. He's enjoying himself."

- "There's not a great deal of money coming in. But we'll find a way to get through it."

- "Ginny wasn't at her best when I saw her. Maybe she had a hangover. I'll call her."

- "The stock market's gone down. In time it'll probably go up again."

- "There's a rumour that the company might have to close. I'd better look around to see what alternative employment I might do, just in case."

- "Things could be better between Bobby and me. I'll talk to him about it."

- "I have a few things to do, but only one of them is really urgent. Another couple are important but not urgent, so they can wait till tomorrow. It doesn't really matter about the others."

- "I'll be interested to see what people have said about what I wrote on Facebook. But it's not the first thing in my life. Life is too short."

- "Somebody insulted me. So what? I am not going to allow myself to be offended. Life is too short to indulge in crappy feelings."

- "Come on! Sabre-toothed tigers haven't been seen near here for more than twenty years!"

Don't believe it? If you believe that bad things are more likely to happen than normal or good things, you can do an experiment! A lady client of mine told me she hated having days off, weekends away or going on holiday, because all the time she would be worrying whether something awful would happen to her son. On normal working days she didn't worry because her mind was otherwise occupied. There was no particular reason for her worry: her son is grown up, healthy and happy, and is not engaged in any hazardous work or pastimes. I proposed she carry out an experiment. It was a national holiday the next day and she was going on a day trip with her husband to such and such a place. Just for one day, I asked her to allow herself not to think about her son. If he came into her mind, she was to let him pass on through, and bring her mind back to the here and now. She did this, no disaster befell her son, and the sky didn't fall in. She actually enjoyed herself. That experiment was just a small step towards learning. But if she carries out this experiment repeatedly, it will gradually begin not to be an experiment any more. It will become her natural behaviour to focus less on fears about her son.

Having replaced a negative thought with a positive one, you can also *choose* how to respond. Whether to...

Avoid the source of the worry. This might mean avoiding talking to a certain person or avoiding certain situations. If you worry about public speaking you might avoid speaking in public. This may not be the ideal kind of response, because for one reason or another you may not be able or want to maintain it.

Adapt to the source of the worry. This might mean you change your behaviour with regard to a certain person or situation. You might, for instance, decide to go on doing talks but make them briefer. Or you might decide that it doesn't matter if you make mistakes or what people think of it.

Act to solve a problem, by practical means if it is a practical problem, or by means of emotional support if it is an emotional one. You might for example, train yourself or get training in public speaking. You might seek reassurance from people who have heard you speak. You might listen to any critical comments constructively and decide to address those issues. If your anxiety is really over the top you could seek cognitive behavioural therapy from a psychologist or counsellor.

Accept that there is nothing you can or want to do, and put your mind at peace.

Remember the 4 'A's: Avoid, Adapt, Act, Accept. They are your choices!

The power to ***choose*** means you are no longer controlled by the worry goblins. It means ***you are in control***. Control gives you self-belief and self-belief makes you worry less.

Nurture Self-Belief

You could also call this 'inner strength'. It is the quiet confidence that you possess the faculties to be able to deal effectively with life. I cannot but skim over a few suggestions here. But I will, skim over them. How can you develop inner strength?

- Maintain and improve your physical health.

- Think positively and be optimistic.

- Listen to and be around positive people. It is contagious.

- Keep a collection of words of wisdom. Some suggestions are given in Chapter 4.

- Recognise your affinities. These are things which deeply enthuse you, make you buzz, or which bring you home to the real you. Things which make you feel more alive. Places, people, things, environments, landscapes, activities. Arrange to have frequent contact with them.

- Seek to know yourself realistically (your strengths and your weaknesses) and seek to evolve as a person. Life is for learning. We are blessed with this opportunity.

- Keep an inner sanctum where you hold your core values and images of your affinities (the things which make you more alive). Make it an inner area of calm, delight and tranquillity. Locate it in your lower abdomen, a three or four inches below your navel. Meditate upon it.

- Believe in something bigger than you. God, a universal consciousness, mother nature, humanity, whatever humps your camel. You are little and the universe is big and mysterious. But you are a unique, wonderful, mysterious instant of this universe!

- Love. Yourself, your acts and endeavours, life, people, this beautiful universe. Every instant we live for the now, acting or interacting with good intentions, true to ourself, as well as we are able, and as though this were the only instant available to us in the whole vastness of time, we express love.

Here is a noble aim: to be able to say, "I am perfectly happy with my place in the universe. What then should I worry about?"

Main Points

- Breathe, meditate, and exercise (healthy body, healthy mind).

- Distract your mind.

- Slow down and get in touch with nature.

- Be practical: rationalise and problem-solve.

- Talk to people.

- Change your mind (thoughts and attitude) – REST:

  - Recognise your negative thoughts.

  - Examine them.

- ○ Stop!
- ○ Take control.
- Nurture self-belief.

How Not to Worry?

4. Words of Wisdom

We can all benefit from the wisdom of others, especially those whose words have inspired and uplifted generations of human beings. Here are some from down through the years, decades and centuries. You don't have to read this in order, you can just dip in and read at random; some may speak to you more than others...

"Care about what other people think of you and you will always be their prisoner."

"Life is a series of natural and spontaneous changes. Don't resist them; that only creates sorrow. Let reality be reality. Let things flow naturally forward in whatever way they like."

"When I let go of what I am, I become what I might be."

"If you are depressed you are living in the past. If you are anxious you are living in the future. If you are at peace you are living in the present."

- Lao Tzu (6th - 4th century BCE)

"Day by day, what you choose, what you think and what you do is who you become."

"No man ever steps in the same river twice, for it's not the same river and he's not the same man."

- *Heraclitus* (c. 535 - 475 BCE)

"If you look into your own heart, and you find nothing wrong there, what is there to worry about? What is there to fear?"

"They must often change, who would be constant in happiness or wisdom."

- Confucius (551 - 479 BCE)

"What we think and ponder upon becomes the inclination of our minds."

"Your worst enemy cannot harm you as much as your own unguarded thoughts."

"The secret of health for both mind and body is not to mourn for the past, worry about the future, or anticipate troubles, but to live in the present moment wisely and earnestly."

- Buddha (c. 480 - c. 400 BCE)

"Beware the barrenness of a busy life."

"He is richest who is content with the least, for contentment is the wealth of nature."

- Socrates (c. 470-399 BCE)

"Courage is knowing what not to fear."

"There are two things a person should never be angry at, what they can help, and what they cannot."

"Nothing in the affairs of men is worthy of great anxiety."

- Plato (c. 428 – c. 347 BCE)

"Probable impossibilities are to be preferred to improbable possibilities."

"Anyone can become angry - that is easy, but to be angry with the right person at the right time, and for the right purpose and in the right way - that is not within everyone's power and that is not easy."

- Aristotle (384 - 322 BCE)

"Formidable is that enemy that lies hid in a man's own breast."

- Publilius Syrus (Syrian writer and freedman of Rome, 85 – 43 BCE)

"As a rule, men worry more about what they can't see than about what they can."

- Julius Caesar (100 - 44 BCE)

"Happy is the man who has broken the chains which hurt the mind, and has given up worrying once and for all."

- Ovid (43 BCE -17/18 CE)

"Anger is an acid that can do more harm to the vessel in which it is stored than to anything on which it is poured."

"True happiness is to enjoy the present without anxious dependence on the future."

"Count each day as a separate life."

- Seneca (4 BCE - 65 CE)

"Who of you by worrying can add a single hour to your life?"

- Luke 12:25-31 (Saint Luke the Evangelist died in the year 84 AD/CE)

"Neither blame nor praise yourself."

"The whole life of a man is but a point in time; let us enjoy it."

- Plutarch (46 - c. 120 CE)

"He is a wise man who does not grieve for the things which he has not, but rejoices for those which he has."

"Make the best use of what's in your power and take the rest as it happens."

"Control thy passions lest they take vengeance on thee."

"The key is to keep company only with people who uplift you, whose presence calls forth your best."

"There is only one way to happiness and that is to cease worrying about things which are beyond the power of our will."

- Epictetus (c. 55 - 135 CE)

"If you are distressed by anything external, the pain is not due to the thing itself, but to your estimate of it; and this you have the power to revoke at any moment."

"Never let the future disturb you. You will meet it, if you have to, with the same weapons of reason which today arm you against the present."

- Marcus Aurelius (121 - 180 CE)

"Solvitur ambulando" (It is solved by acting).

- Augustine of Hippo (354 - 430 CE)

"No amount of guilt can change the past, and no amount of worrying can change the future."

- Umar Ibn Al-Khattaab (Muslim caliph, 584 - 644 CE)

"If the problem can be solved why worry? If the problem cannot be solved worrying will do you no good."

- Shantideva (8th-century Indian Buddhist monk)

"The moonbeam splinters night's skirt with light, drink wine, there is no better time than this."[5]

- Omar Khayyam (1048 – 1131)

"A human being has so many skins inside, covering the depths of the heart. We know so many things, but we don't know ourselves! Why, thirty or forty skins or hides, as thick and hard as an ox's or bear's, cover the soul. Go into your own ground and learn to know yourself there."

- Meister Eckhart (German theologian, c. 1260 – c. 1328)

Dans ses écrits, un sage Italien
Dit que le mieux est l'ennemi du bien.

A wise Italian wrote
The best is the enemy of the good.

- Voltaire (1694 - 1778) in "La Bégueule"

"Do not anticipate trouble, or worry about what may never happen. Keep in the sunlight."

- Benjamin Franklin (1705 - 1790)

---

5   "Drink wine" is supposed to be taken metaphorically here, although I'll leave that up to you (but moderation please, wine is a pleasure, not a medication!).

"He is rich who owns the day, and no one owns the day who allows it to be invaded with fret and anxiety."

- Ralph Waldo Emerson (American essayist, lecturer, philosopher, and poet, 1803 - 1882)

"Worry is rust upon the blade."

- Henry Ward Beecher (American clergyman, 1813-1887)

It matters not how strait the gate,
How charged with punishments the scroll,
I am the master of my fate:
I am the captain of my soul.

- William Ernest Henley (1849-1903) in "Invictus"

"I am an old man and have known a great many troubles, but most of them have never happened."

"Drag your thoughts away from your troubles... by the ears, by the heels, or any other way you can manage it."

- Mark Twain (1835 - 1910)

"The greatest mistake you can make in life is to be continually fearing you will make one."

- Elbert Hubbard (American writer, publisher, artist, and philosopher, 1856-1915)

"If you believe that feeling bad or worrying long enough will change a past or future event, then you are residing on another planet with a different reality system."

- William James (American philosopher and psychologist, 1842-1910)

"Worry is a thin stream of fear trickling through the mind. If encouraged, it cuts a channel into which all other thoughts are drained."

- Arthur Somers Roche (American author, 1883-1935)

"People become attached to their burdens sometimes more than the burdens are attached to them."

- George Bernard Shaw (1856 – 1950)

"Most people spend more time and energy going around problems than in trying to solve them."

- Henry Ford (1863 - 1947)

"Let our advance worrying become advance thinking and planning."

- Winston Churchill (1874 - 1965)

"I can go without good food, but I can't live without seeing green leaves and beautiful flowers. Every flower here is a symbol of paradise."

- Mohammad Kabir (Gardener in Kabul, 2014)[6]

"Worry often gives a small thing a big shadow."

- Swedish Proverb

---

6 A report in the Sunday Times on 15th June 2014, told the story of Mohammad Kabir, 102, who had spent over 90 years lovingly tending the garden of the now ruined Darul Aman palace in Kabul: https://www.thetimes.co.uk/article/im-102-and-i-pray-for-a-rosy-afghan-future-92bj3grrxgw (last accessed 7th April 2020).

"You see injuries like that and then you come home and you hear people in Tesco whingeing about this, that and the other. You just want to say, "Oh my God, have you any idea?"

- Squadron Leader Charlotte Thompson-Edgar (Army medic, 2015)[7]

"If a problem is fixable, if a situation is such that you can do something about it, then there is no need to worry. If it's not fixable, then there is no help in worrying. There is no benefit in worrying whatsoever."

"As a human being, anger is a part of our mind. Irritation also part of our mind. But you can do - anger come, go. Never keep in your sort of - your inner world, then create a lot of suspicion, a lot of distrust, a lot of negative things, more worry."

- Dalai Lama

---

7   The Sunday Times of 1st March 2015 carried an article about an RAF nurse and paramedic called Charlotte Thompson-Edgar. Squadron Leader Thompson-Edgar was awarded a Victoria Cross in recognition not only of her "exceptional performance" in six tours to Afghanistan, but also the "great skill, courage and determination" she showed in saving a badly injured soldier in difficult circumstances. She had used a pioneering medical technique in an ingenious and unconventional way to save the soldier, who had lost 75% of his blood.

"Tension is who you think you should be. Relaxation is who you are."

- Chinese proverb